Facebook Marketing in 2019 Made (Stupidly) Easy

Vol.3 of the "Small Business Marketing Made (Stupidly) Easy" Collection

by Michael Clarke

Founder, Punk Rock Marketing

Published in USA by: Punk Rock Marketing

Michael Clarke

© Copyright 2018

ISBN-13: 978-1-970119-12-1

Table of Contents

Chapter 6: Creating a Facebook Ad Strategy That Doesn't Suck (and Actually Makes You Money) 90

Chapter 7: How to Use Content Ads to Boost Your Brand (and Bottom Line)............. 103

Chapter 8: How to Get Super-Cheap Leads With Facebook Video Ads 124

Chapter 9: Facebook Retargeting Ads...The Final (Profitable) Frontier....................142

About the Author

Michael Clarke is a former cubicle monkey turned social media marketing consultant and author. He is also the owner of the world's most neurotic Jack Russell Terrier.

Also By Michael Clarke

TWITTER MARKETING IN 2019 MADE (STUPIDLY) EASY

VIDEO MARKETING IN 2019 MADE STUPIDLY EASY

PINTEREST MARKETING IN 2019 MADE STUPIDLY EASY

INSTAGRAM MARKETING IN 2019 MADE STUPIDLY EASY

LINKEDIN MARKETING IN 2019 MADE STUPIDLY EASY

EMAIL MARKETING IN 2019 MADE STUPIDLY EASY

SEARCH ENGINE OPTIMIZATION IN 2019 MADE STUPIDLY EASY

A Special FREE Gift for You!

If you'd like FREE instant access to my seminar "How to Make a Damn Good Living With Social Media (Even If You Hate Social Media" then head over to **PunkRockMarketing.com/Free**. (What else you gonna do? Watch another "Twilight" movie?!)

Prologue: Yeah, But How Do You Make Money With Facebook?

Just so you know, this isn't one of those books that will tell you how to "connect" or be "authentic" on Facebook.

Truth is, I hate Facebook.

I hate "engaging" with annoying friends from high school who share every single photo of their zip-lining vacation in Costa Rica. (Especially when I'm sitting at a desk. Working.) I hate "connecting" with my cousin's weekly political rant on what's wrong with Washington politics.

Can't stand "being authentic" on a media

platform that barrages me with "Bubble Safari" requests and "Mafia Wars" clues and "You Should Like This Crappy Page Because Your Friends Liked This Crappy Page" suggestions.

Facebook is annoying, shallow, pretentious, invasive…

And that's why it pains me to say this: for reaching the largest, most targeted customer base ANYWHERE — at the cheapest, lowest ad cost — nothing works like Facebook.

"Always Be Selling"

If you're reading this book, chances are you fall into one of two categories:

1. **You've tried Facebook in the past,** had lousy results, wasted a bunch of time and money and don't know what the fuss is all about. *But other people seem to do well with Facebook marketing and you want to know their secret.*

2.   You've avoided Facebook like the plague. You think it's a technological fad that creates a lot of marketplace noise but doesn't lead to sustainable profits. *But other people seem to do well with Facebook and you want to know their secret.*

Either way, you've come to the right place.

There's no better evangelist than the converted, and I have swung from hating (nearly) everything about a company who turned "friend" into a verb and designed their entire color scheme around the fact their CEO is color blind…

…to understanding that Facebook is poised to become THE tool that people use to do nearly everything.

Not just A tool.

THE tool.

Facebook is going after every part of your experience. (How you search on the Internet, buy products, read books, watch movies, find restaurants, check out those photos of that girl you had a crush on in high school, etc.)

And if they accomplish just 10% of what they want to, they'll be an overbearing, intrusive, obnoxious presence in our lives for decades to come.

And one that we as marketers can use for our own benefit.

The Magic Formula

So, the big dilemma about Facebook marketing comes down to this...how do all of those "likes" and "friends" and "pages" and "posts" lead to actual customers?

The process is simple. It goes a little something like this:

1. Create content that doesn't suck (and doesn't put people into a coma)

2. Build a Facebook Page that doesn't suck

3. Attract people to like and follow your pages and posts

4. Send these fans (and non-fans) to

content that lives on your site

5.   Retarget these folks with Facebook ads

6.   Rinse and Repeat…and count your money

That's what I'm going to show you in this book. Step by step.

I've replicated this system in a bunch of different markets, with a bunch of different customer segments. And the only time I haven't had success is when I've deviated from this formula. (Or skipped a step because I was lazy.)

So, if you don't mind, we're gonna leave the talk about "connecting" and "being authentic" for the other guys (and girls).

We're just going to talk about what works. And kick some serious Facebook marketing ass in the process.

You ready?

Chapter 1:
5 Ways to Find Rocket Fuel for Your Fan Page

"All things are ready, if our mind be so."
-William Shakespeare

Before we jump into the nitty-gritty of creating your Facebook fan page — and there is quite a bit of nit and grit — it's good to create a reserve of that most valuable Facebook marketing resource…content.

I know what you're gonna say: "Content? But I want to create a zombie army of Facebook fans who do my bidding and buy my crap."

Sounds like you've been drinking the Facebook Kool-Aid from 2010. (Ya know, the good, old days when you could post something on Facebook and actual humans would see it.)

The trouble is, these days, getting people (and that includes your own fans) to see the content you put out on Facebook is just slightly harder than finding a Transformers movie that doesn't suck.

Gone are the days when we could just post a silly "fill in the blank" question and get 35 comments — "The person I'd least like to see President is______."

We must be more strategic. Thoughtful. Super-ninja.

The good news is most marketers on Facebook, and that includes your competition, are still doing things the old way. (Wave to them as you zoom past them in the sales charts.)

But it all starts with creating CONTENT that doesn't suck. (That we can then use to boost engagement on our page — and attract leads into our funnel.)

So, here are the Five Pillars of Non-Sucky Content Every Business on Facebook Should Have:

Non-Sucky Piece of Facebook Content #1: A Killer Blog Post (With a # in the Title)

I know. Blog post? What 19th-century rock did I crawl out from under?

Don't I know we live in a post-selfie world where everybody Snapchats and Vines their way through life.

Here's the thing: SOME people prefer to learn about a topic through words. (Not just Instagram posts.)

And studies have shown if somebody READS more than 75% of your blog post, they are 10x more likely to become a lead, and 5x more likely to be a customer.

Now, a blog post doesn't have to be a 5,000-

word essay about tax annuities. (Though it can be.)

A killer blog post can be things like a:

- How-to article walking the reader through an important topic

- Interview with a notable person in your industry

- Collection of YouTube videos around a specific theme (Even videos you didn't create)

- Excerpts from blog columns/posts (you didn't write) around a specific theme (Be sure to ask permission)

- List of recommended resources

- Case study showing results you or your clients have gotten

- "Best Of…" post (this can be on almost anything)

- Mission Statement/Declaration (In which you say "you're mad as hell…" about something in your industry and "you will not take it anymore")

Whatever you think will cause your target audience to sit up — take notice — and click on your post as they scroll through their Facebook newsfeed on their smart phone is the way to go.

And if you're able to weave a "#" in your blog post, all the better. There's just something about "#s" that calms the brain and reassures people that a task is manageable. For instance, which would you rather read: "How to Survive a Tax Audit" or "5 Secrets to Surviving Tax Audit."

Neither is pleasant, but I'll bet you'd rather read the "5 Secrets" one. (And if you do happen to know how to survive a tax audit, I'm all ears.)

Non-Sucky Piece of Facebook Content #2: A Killer Video (That Explains Something in a Fun, Interactive Way)

Now, once ya got your blog post created, it's time to appeal to the 91% other people out there…with a killer video that explains a confusing/important topic in a fun, interactive way.

Don't worry, this video doesn't have to be super long. (These days, anything over three minutes feels longer than a "Lord of the Rings" movie.)

But you want your video to cover ONE single topic exhaustively. (Don't tease at a solution, give people what they need to know.)

And try to put yourself (or someone on your team) in the video. (Either by talking straight at the camera or using a white board to explain something.)

If you have a brick-and-mortar store, you could also do something where you walk people through your shop. (The "Dollar Shave Club" guys do this brilliantly.)

Just resist the urge to do a screen capture video where you ramble over a Power Point presentation. (These. Are. Boring.)

And when you figure out the topic you're gonna cover, here's how I recommend you structure your video:

1.   **Start by asking people to click on the**

video as you point downwards. (" Click to hear the video! Click to hear the video!") I know this is weird, but this will encourage folks to click on your video as they scroll past on their phones.)

2. **Introduce yourself and yer topic.** (" Hi, this is Michael Clarke, author of Facebook Marketing Made (Stupidly) Easy and in this video I'm gonna talk about the microchip that Mark Zuckerberg is trying to implant in your brain.")

3. **Go through the step-by-step instruction and content of your video**. This is the part people are there for.

4. **Give 'em action steps for what to do next.** ("First, you remove the microchip…")

5. **Congratulate them for already acting

even if they haven't. (''And presto! You are now microchip-free.'')

6.   **Thank them for watching and ask them to "like" the video.** (''Thanks for your time and if you'd be so kind to 'like' this video I promise to be your best friend.'')

7.   **Give them your offer!** (''And if you'd like a free copy of my 'Removing the Chip' eBook just head over...'')

And that's it!

Please, don't over-think this. This isn't rocket surgery, as my Dad would say. Just a killer piece of video content - that you can use to awesome (and totally nefarious) means with your Facebook marketing.

Non-Sucky Piece of Facebook Content #3: 5 Touchy-Feely Images of Inspirational Quotes

You probably already know what these are: those motivational quotes you find ALL OVER social media where somebody slaps some inspirational words over a colored background. (Or a view of a sunset. God, how they love sunsets.)

And I find these as inspiring as a late-night infomercial. But I am in the vast minority. (These are like Facebook catnip, people love 'em.)

So, here's how you make 'em:

- Type into Google "Quotes about (insert adjective related to your business)" and collect FIVE quotes (along with the speaker.) If in doubt just do something about adversity or perseverance. Everybody wants to overcome that.
- Head over to Canva. Totally FREE

photo-editing tool. Perfect for creating quotes.

- Choose "Facebook Post" size as your template.
- Choose a neutral, colored background that catches your eye. Nothing too dark or too light.
- Add text boxes, and type in the quote and the person who uttered it.

Export…and you're good to go!

Non-Sucky Piece of Facebook Content #4: 5 Links to Funny Articles/Videos

I know you THINK what your fans really want is to read those erudite 10,000-word essays you found on the "New Republic" Twitter feed.

But the truth is most people are stressed-out and tired and just want something funny, dumb and silly while they're in the bathroom at work.

And if you're able to churn out at least one of

these a week, your fans will realize your page isn't just there to sell crap and "educate." Your page is fun! (Even if it really isn't.)

Some of my favorite go-to places to find stuff like this is:

- PopUrls - Pretty much a "best of" containing the coolest - and weirdest - the Internet has to offer.

- BuzzFeed - Most of their stuff is outright click bait, but sometimes you'll find a funny piece of content or two you can share with your tribe.

- The Onion - I frickin' love "The Onion." ("Mom Thinks You'd Enjoy Restaurant She Can't Remember the Name Of.") Their stuff is always good for a chuckle or seven. (And perfect for sharing in your Facebook feed.)

- AllTop - This site is like the NY public library of the Internet. (Where everything is categorized and rated by actual humans.) Perfect for a targeted little piece of content here and there. (Best of all, you can set up RSS feeds so you'll be notified when new content, fitting your area of expertise, pops up.)

Non-Sucky Piece of Facebook Content #5: 5 Super-Simple (No-Brainer) Questions Your Tribe Can Answer

There was a time, way back in the Mesozoic era (or what we call 2010) when every Facebook page out there would fill their news feeds with this social media sludge. ("Reeses or Snickers?")

And though they aren't quite as effective as they used to be, they still have a place. (Especially for boosting the popularity of your page.)

The key is to use questions that have "some" connection to your brand. ("My favorite horror movie is___?" is a great fit for my screenwriter audience, not so much for my golf

tribe.)

So, here are a couple of my favorite go-to's when trying to find brain-dead questions so simple even a Kardashian can answer them:

- "My favorite (insert) is ___?"
- What's your biggest frustration/gripe about ___?
- What's one word that describes ___?
- Write a caption to a photo.
- Trivia questions.
- "(This) or (that)?"
- "If you were trapped on a desert island and could choose only one (insert)…what would it be?"

I know these are pandering. But for what you're asking this content to do — get Facebook users past their overpowering laziness and type words on a screen — they are devastatingly effective.

And as with all these forms of content rocket fuel, they're perfect for attracting new fans and distracting your existing ones from the fact that you're eventually gonna sell them something.

Which is what we'll cover in the next chapter.

Chapter One Key Takeaways:

- **Having one killer blog post can go a long way towards not only connecting with your existing fans but attracting new fans.** (Note: Blog posts don't have to mean boring, 5000-word essays. They can be things like "best of" columns, curated video, case studies, and resource lists.)

- **One killer video is not only an awesome way to reach people who would otherwise never read your blog post**, but it can also be the vehicle for some of the cheapest (and most effective) advertising on the Internet. (More on that later.)

- **Images with touchy-feely, motivational quotes STILL do well as Facebook page content.** Despite the author's best efforts to remove them from the Facebook-verse.

- **Funny videos/articles are perfect for entertaining your stressed-out, totally bored tribe.** (And they get your fans to look forward to your future Facebook posts.)

- **No-brainer questions aren't quite as effective as they used to be**, but they're still perfect for boosting the "engagement" of your page. (Which Facebook uses in their witchcraft algorithms, so they're kinda important.)

Chapter 2:
6 Keys to a Profitable Facebook Sales Machine

"There is no one giant step that does it. It's a lot of little steps."

-Peter A. Cohen

I know you're champing at the bit to get your Facebook page of unstoppable profit awesomeness up and running…and we're gonna get to it. Promise!

But I'd like to encourage you to begin at the end and work backwards. (Like all those "self-help" books tell you to.)

Don't worry, I'm not gonna ask you to do any

mantras. We're just gonna set up the foundational goodies you'll need to turn those likes and fans into cold, hard cash.

Because "engagement" and "branding" sound great, but it doesn't keep the lights on. (Unless your landlord is a lot more flexible than mine.)

So, here are 6 Keys to Setting Up the Ultimate Facebook Sales Machine:

Facebook Sales Machine Element #1: Facebook Retargeting Code on ALL Your WebPages

Facebook retargeting code? What's that? (Does it involve Wookies and the Millennium Falcon?)

No.

Retargeting code is simply a batch of nonsensical gibberish that lets you "remarket" to folks weeks, if not months, after they've visited a page on your website.

This is how, after you look at a product page on

a website, ads for that very product seem to "follow" you all around the Internet.

Aside from the obvious "Big Brother" connotations, remarketing is a super-powerful strategy. (And one that can cut your lead acquisition cost by 50%.)

But, for now, all you gotta do is:

- **Generate your Facebook pixel.** (Head over to PunkRockMarketing.com/FacebookPixel for a walk-through of how to do this.)
- **Have your web designer - or local neighborhood 12-year-old hacker - install it on every page of your website.** (Especially those email capture and thank you pages hosted on other platforms.)
- **Count your money** like Scrooge McDuck.

Okay, we're not quite at the "Scrooge McDuck"

phase…yet. (But we will be when we get to Chapter 7.)

Just know you have now taken a first step in a much larger world. (You didn't think I was gonna let that "Star Wars" thing go, did you?)

Facebook Sales Machine Element #2: A Freebie Thing-a-majiggy That Doesn't Suck

No matter what yer business model is, the best way to attract leads (who hopefully become lifelong customers) is to offer prospects some kind of freebie or special offer in exchange for an email address.

Unfortunately, many of the freebies/special offers that businesses offer are:

- Vague
- Overwhelming
- Cliché (Been done to death)
- Underwhelming (Doesn't promise big results)

- Boring

So, here are a couple of tips to keep in mind when creating (or refining) your freebie/special offer:

- **Solve one problem (or satisfy one desire.)** Don't offer an eBook that covers every aspect of a topic, or a coupon that offers 10% off anything on the menu. Have the eBook solve ONE problem ("My #1 Secret to Buying a Used Car") or have the coupon offer a discount on one item ("Get 25% Off All Lobster Dishes on Thursdays After a Full Moon.") The confused mind says no, so don't let 'em get confused.

- **Video ain't as awesome as it used to be.** There was a time when people offering "video tutorials" was a big deal. (Mostly because nobody had any idea how they did it.) But these days it just ain't that impressive and watching a video "sounds" like work. PDF's and audio formats not only sound like high value, but they're easy to consume too.

- **If offering information, make it sound secretive.** Cheat sheets. Insider guides. Toolkits. Resource Lists. Anything that sounds like you're saving people a crap load of time — and offering them something other people don't know about — is a good thing.

- **If offering a coupon, choose the discount that "sounds" higher.** "Save 50% off" sounds a heckuva lot better than "Save $.43." Do some testing to see which works best with your audience.

- **Free trials work great for software and monthly programs.** Not just because most people forget to cancel. But because it lowers the bar of resistance and shows you have confidence in your product.

- **Scarcity is a powerful Mofo**. If you can instill some kind of limited-time period — especially for a discount — that can work staggeringly well. (Later we'll go over how to use Facebook contests.)

- **Don't spend HOURS working on your freebie and/or coupon**. You'll probably have to change it in a year anyway…so don't spend YEARS crafting the perfect freebie. Just get it done and get it

Facebook Sales Machine Element #3: A Short Video "Selling" Your Freebie

Huh? A video "selling" the freebie? What is this craziness I'm having you do now?

Relax. This video is only gonna be about 90

seconds long. But it might be the most important (and profitable) part of your Facebook sales machine.

Because eventually we're gonna "show" this video to warm prospects and it should literally help your lead costs nose-dive.

Now, in Chapter 8 I go over my entire step-by-step outline for how to create this pre-sell video. (So, no need to create it right this minute.)

But for the time being, think about how you might answer the following questions:

1. Who's the best person for our business to put on camera to talk about our business? (Skip photogenic, go for passionate.)

2. What pain point does my product/service solve?

3. What are the main obstacles standing in the way of our customers solving this problem? (What beliefs or habits get in their way of success.)

4. Can the person on video talk about their OWN experience or connection to the product/service? (Beyond..."Hey, I'm getting paid to talk about this!")

This video can be as short as 60 seconds or as long as 2 minutes. (Or even LONGER if the offer warrants it — things like a webinar sign-up may need more information.)

And don't worry about making it perfect. Just make it honest. And human. (Even if the aliens are controlling your brain.)

Facebook Sales Machine Element #4: A Landing Page That Doesn't Suck

This is probably the SECOND most important element of your Facebook sales machine, and that is having a landing page that doesn't suck.

And by "doesn't suck," I simply mean: a webpage that converts. (Industry standard is about 25% — though the tips I'm about to share should probably boost that well above 40%.)

So, how do we achieve this? Well, after testing this a ton (and making every landing page mistake in the book) I've found good landing pages have the following elements:

- **A picture of the FREE thing yer giving away** (Such as a book cover or coupon graphic — you can get this done on Fiverr)

- **A headline that makes it clear WHO this freebie is for** — ("Attention golf instructors"; "To All Denver Oral Surgeons!")

- **An emotional, action-packed description of what the free thing is** and what subscribers will get if they opt-in) — ("Download my FREE report "7 Ways to Offer a Free Report" and You'll learn my secret strategies for boosting your profits 1300%!)

- **A button they can click** to enter their

info

And that's about it!

Unfortunately achieving this through a simple WordPress template - or HTML coding - can be difficult and expensive. (Especially if you hire designer.)

I recommend the following tools:

- LeadPages (The tool I use)
- Instapage

Both are good tools for letting you use pre-built, mobile-responsive templates to create landing pages that look super killer.

I prefer LeadPages because they give you conversion stats about your pages right there in the dash. (No need to keep checking Google Analytics.) But InstaPage is good too.

And the COOL thing is you can use this same tool to create a killer "Thank You" page where you can sell your stuff RIGHT AWAY.

Facebook Sales Machine Element #5: A Way to Collect and Send Emails

So, I'm not gonna spend a ton of time on this, because chances are you've already got some email collection (and email sending) tool in your arsenal.

But in case you don't.... I highly, highly recommend you get one. (They're vital for establishing long-term relationships with your customers and creating offers that can cut through the social media noise and get noticed.)

There are a lot of players in this space. I use ConvertKit, mostly because it gives you most of the features of a $1000/month platform, at a fraction of the cost.

But you could just as easily use a service like iContact or MailChimp. They're all good, they're all cheap. And they're all essential.

Whichever way you go, choose something. (You'll regret it if you don't.)

Facebook Sales Machine Element #6: Obnoxious (But Effective) Opt-In Crap on Your Website

The last piece of the Facebook Sales Machine puzzle is to have lead-capture mechanisms in place for when people visit your website.

Now some of these are simple to execute, and other require more technical know-how. (If you're not sure how to do any of this just find a talented, unemployed hacker on Fiverr to do it.

Here are methods I recommend:

- **Right sidebar lead-capture widget —** This is a simple vertical widget placed on every page of your blog or website. (Or wherever you think is appropriate.) You don't even have to design it, just use your email service to create the code and then place it on your site.

- **Blog post footer widget —** Here's one

most folks forget about. And that is have a horizontal widget at the end of each of your blog posts or articles touting your latest freebie. (Best of all, once you create this you can put it anywhere you want — including in the middle of long articles.)

- **Obnoxious Exit Pop (Optional)** — Okay, so this one is on the spammy side. But this is where you install an exit-pop plugin on your site that forces people to "confirm" they want to leave your website and give them one last chance to opt in. Spammy? Yes. Effective? Absolutely! Something that will piss people off and lower your opt-in rates? Not even close.

Chapter Two Key Takeaways:

- **Having Facebook retargeting code installed on your website will save you a lot of wasted energy** — and put money directly in your pocket.

- **Successful Facebook marketing requires a freebie (or offer) that doesn't suck.** Keep it specific, easy to consume, and quick to produce. (Don't spend years on it.)

- **Creating a short video that "sells" your freebie is one of the smartest (and most effective) things you can do for your Facebook marketing.** Don't forget to a) encourage people to click b) establish your authority c) get right to their pain point d) offer a solution and e) tell 'em to click in the post.

- **Ya gotta have a landing page that

doesn't suck to make this whole thing work. And that means having a picture of your freebie, a headline that tells folks who the freebie is for, body text that tells people what they'll get, and a button they can click.

- **This whole Facebook Sales Machine needs a way to collect email addresses** and send out pre-generated emails. I use ConvertKit, but you can use any tool you like.

- **Don't forget to add lead-capture opportunities into your website design.** Right sidebar widgets and blog post footer widgets are must-haves. (And if you can stomach the possible "spammy nature" of them, exit-pop plugins are devastatingly effective.)

Chapter 3: The Ultimate Facebook Fan-Page Makeover

"When all the details fit in perfectly, something is probably wrong with the story."
-Charles Baxter

I wish I could tell you looks don't matter. I wish I could tell you lots of things.

But how your Facebook Fan Page looks — how cool, fun and relevant to your audience your page appears to be — makes a huge difference in the success of your Facebook marketing.

So, before we get likes and fans and (more importantly) customers, we will need to pimp out our Facebook fan page to make it sleek, modern and one kick-ass lead-generatin' machine.

Note: If you've been living under a zombie-proof bunker for the last six years — and don't have a Facebook page yet — head over to Facebook.com/Pages and "Create a page".)

So, here's my Five-Step Facebook Makeover checklist to help your Fan page look like you spent thousands of dollars on getting it designed, for just the price of a latte:

Facebook Page Makeover Step No. 1: Choose a Facebook Page Name (and Username) That Doesn't Suck

Page Name Vs. Username. This one always confuses. (And no wonder, they sound exactly the same. Thanks, Facebook!)

Here's the deal: Your "Page Name" is the name that shows up right next to your profile thumbnail on your Fan Page.

Below the Page Name is the number of likes and

number of people talking about your page.

It is also the name that will show up when you run ads to either boost your number of likes or promoting content.

So, it's very important.

Your Facebook Username, on the other hand, is what is in the actual URL of your page: http://Facebook.com/MyUsername.

So, here's what I recommend for USERNAMES:

- **Choose something you're comfortable having on your business card.** I find with most of my clients, the Fan Page ranks well ahead of my actual website in the search-engine results. So, it's good to go with something you like the sound of.

- **Try to avoid hyphens or underscores if you can.** Not always possible, but it makes it a lot easier for your page to get found if the "page name" doesn't have these.

- **Beg, borrow, and steal your way to 25 likes for your Page.** Until you got your 25 likes, you'll have to stick with an abysmal username like Facebook.com/profile.php?id=52984566. So, once you choose a username, get those 25 likes as soon as you can.

- **Choosing a Facebook username is like having children.** Once you have 'em, you have 'em for life. So, choose wisely.

- **If somebody grabbed your username, and it does happen, choose something else related to your business**. Facebook doesn't check to see if usernames match the pages. They don't care. They are Facebook. So, if somebody grabbed "PlumbingPatrol" and that was the actual name of my business, then I might go local, such as

"SanDiegoPlumbers" or "PlumbersSanDiego" or even do something more broad such as "BestPlumberSanDiego" or "FindAPlumber."

Okay, that's USERNAMES. Now let's turn to your PAGE NAME:

- **Get a keyword in there if you can.** You can get some serious SEO Google juice from your Fan Page. So, try to get a keyword in there subtly. Not: *Joe's Pizza - Best Denver Pizza, Best Denver Italian, Best Calzone Denver"* but *"Joe's Pizza - Best Denver Pizza"* would be fine.

- **Don't force a keyword in there if it doesn't sound right**. There's nothing worse than a Fan Page that sounds like a keyword factory. (Always ask…would my customers be into this?)

- **If branding isn't important, then go

with something "fun" and "personal." If getting your business name in there isn't crucial, then go with something like "I Love French Press Coffee" or "BBQ Grill Gurus" or "Bull Riding News." Remember Facebook is all about fun, social activity. (Not just a place to sell your crap.)

- **You can create as many Facebook Pages as you want.** If your business caters to different audiences, you may want to create separate Fan pages for these segments and take advantage of the SEO boost some keyword-laced page names can offer. (I worked with a law firm who created a separate Facebook page for each of their divisions, such as "bankruptcy"; "DUI" and "personal injury.")

- **You can only change your page name if you've got fewer than 200**

likes. So, choose carefully and get this whole Page Name nailed down before you get too popular. Trust me, by following the tips in this book, you'll get to 200 likes in no time, so neglect this tip at your own peril.

Facebook Page Makeover Step No. 2: Put Keywords (Almost) Everywhere

So, we've talked about some SEO benefits that a few well-placed keywords in your username and Fan Page name can do for you.

But here's where the real SEO magic happens. Lucky for us, it's an area where most marketers fail to take advantage of — the "informational" fields that are all over your Facebook Fan Page.

This includes your:

- "About" section
- "Description"
- "Short description"

-     "Products" field

To update these fields on your Fan page, simply click "edit page" and then select the "basic information" tab.

Now, you don't want to go overboard. You don't want to say:

"Drain Patrol is a Modesto plumber you can trust. When it comes to choosing a Modesto plumber, Drain Patrol should be your first call. We have many Modesto plumbers at your service."

Sounds like somebody drank a bottle of Nyquil before writing that.

But you want to sprinkle in keywords your customers might use to "find" you.

*"We specialize in **data recovery**," "Jimmy Cobra voted #1 **LA Tattoo artist**," "Looking for **Pittsburgh Steeler Jerseys**? Steeler Town has got 'em all."*

If I was trying to include "Denver tax preparer" in my "about" section, I might do something like:

"John Smith is a dedicated Denver tax preparer whose sole mission is to help people reach their financial goals, build

for their economic future and defraud the IRS."

Quick Tip: Don't forget to include your website in the very first part of your "About" Section. This is the most visible area for you to include a link on your Facebook Fan Page. And can lead to lots of additional traffic back to your own website.

Facebook Page Makeover Step No. 3: Create a Timeline Cover Photo That Doesn't Suck

I don't encourage small-biz types to spend a ton of time on the creative for their social media profiles. But Facebook is different.

So much of the real estate on your Facebook fan page is devoted to photos. (Facebook knows most people are lazy and hate to read.)

And there's one photo you need to focus on. That's the Timeline cover photo — the image at the very top of your fan page that stretches horizontally over the entire width of your page.

And it's important.

It's like your very own 24-hour billboard.

(Without the spendy rental costs.)

So, here are tips to crush it with your Fan Page Timeline Photo:

- **Use a photo-heavy design that incorporates the vibe of your company.** And by vibe, I don't mean your boring conference room. What is the mission of your company; what feelings do you hope to convey to your customers; what's the core benefit of your products or services? Put that in your photo.

- **Unless you have an inner graphic designer in you, hire an outside designer to make this photo awesome and not sucky.** Upwork and Fiverr are great places to find talent for super cheap.

- **Add text and calls-to-action — but sparingly.** Couple years ago, Facebook removed the restriction about having no more than 20% text in your Timeline cover pics. (Thank God.) But don't go overboard. Just have your text focused on one action you want folks to take.

- **Make sure the photo is right-aligned and NOT left-aligned.** This just means you want all the action of the photo happen on the RIGHT side. (And not on the left side where it'll get gobbled up by your thumbnail photo.)

- **Pick warm colors (red, brown, orange).** Anything that contrasts with the LA Dodgers color scheme Facebook forces upon the world.

- **Unless your brand is instantly

recognizable, include a tag line that tells us what your company does. So, your company is named Marketing Mojo, but what the hell does that mean? If it's not clear from your company name, add a bit of tag line, something like: "Training, Support, Solutions" or "Your Social Media Sherpa."

- **If relevant, add in testimonials (along with head shots) of your customers.** Social proof is HUGE. And having that baked in to your timeline photo can do absolute wonders.

- **Create a new cover photo for any upcoming promotions, events or product launches.** Got an upcoming webinar? Or a new mini-course you're teaching? Or maybe a live conference event you're organizing? Create a new cover photo to act as a billboard for your shiny new thing you're promoting.

Fan-Page Makeover Step No. 4: Create a Profile Photo That Doesn't Suck

The profile photo is the small thumbnail in the Timeline Cover Photo, on the lower left-hand side. While it doesn't have the sheer "Look at Me, and All of This Cool Stuff I Can Sell You" potential that the Timeline cover photo does…

…it does have a valuable function.

It quickly separates you from the rest of the pack in your fans' newsfeeds. (And most of the time your fans will see this 90% more than they do your timeline cover photo.)

So here are some best practices when it comes to creating a killer profile pic:

- **Start with a quality photo.** Sounds like a no-brainer. But I'm still shocked by how many people use a less-than-stellar pic for their profile spot. (Make sure to upload a square image.)

- **Go with a shot of a person if you can.** Unless you're a huge company, I always recommend going with a head shot over a brand logo. (You are trying to sneak into the news feed, and logos scream "I'm a business who wants you to buy stuff so don't worry about reading me.")

- **When in doubt, go with images over words.** This profile pic will eventually be sized down to 160x160px, so if you can't see your great verbiage at that size, you should probably remove it from the picture altogether.

- **Don't keep changing your profile**

pic. The timeline cover photo can/should be changed frequently. But once you hone in on a good profile pic, stick with it.

Fan-Page Makeover Step No. 5: Add Your Company's Greatest Hits to Your Facebook Timeline

Everyone loves a good success story. And that includes your Facebook fans.

For some unknown reason, people like to scroll through fan pages to find out about the history of a company. (Sounds boring but trust me, people do this.)

And not only that, but these milestones can be a great way to send traffic back to your own website.

So, it behooves you to take a few minutes to brainstorm 8 or 10 key milestones for your company.

These could include:

- The day your company opened its

doors.

- The day your company reached a certain profit threshold.

- The day your company served a famous (ish) person, or a specific-numbered customer.

- Products or services you launched.

- Key partnerships you entered into or huge contracts you were a part of.

- Employees who joined the team.

- Awards your company won.

- Special events your business was a part of.

- Key events in your local community. (Charity stuff works well here.)

So, what do you do when you've got your list of "milestones?" Well, here's what I do:

- **Find a LARGE photo that corresponds to the milestone.**

1200x628 px is the ideal size for these milestone pics, so BIGGER is always BETTER.

- **Add your milestone to your Fan Page Timeline**. To do this, just click on "Offer/Event" in the status update bar of your page, and then select milestone. (Include a keyword, if you can, in the event or story fields.)

- **Add a CTA (call-to-action) in the "Story" field.** (Example: "Here's a picture from my first seminar. (When I had more hair.) To check out our brand-new marketing seminars, head over to http://coolwebsite.com/seminars.")

Chapter Three Key Takeaways:

- **One of the most important makeovers you can do for your Page is to come up with a username and page name that doesn't suck.** You want to aim for a blend of branding, SEO and something that appeals to humans.

- **Facebook pages offer a myriad of SEO keyword opportunities.** This includes some under-utilized areas like "descriptions", "about me" sections, "products", and "company overviews."

- **Create a kick-ass (left-aligned) Timeline cover photo that captures the vibe of your company.** And highlights any important calls-to-action or upcoming events you've got going.

- **Facebook profile photos should be of actual human beings, if possible, and high quality.** (No shaky cell phone pics.)

- **Create a "greatest hits" of your business on your Facebook Timeline.** (It's not self-serving, it's interesting to your customers.) Be sure to incorporate corresponding photos and stories. (And stuff involving employees and humans is always more interesting than product shots.)

- **Facebook apps are a great way to replicate whatever you've got on your website** — such as a menu, video, shopping cart, opt-in form — on your Fan Page. Just try off-loading the app creation to somebody who likes that tech crap.

Chapter 4:

Getting Your First 1000 Fans (in 60 Seconds or Less)

"Only one man in a thousand is a leader of men — the other 999 follow women."

-Groucho Marx

Okay, maybe it'll take longer than 60 seconds. (Might take as long as 90 seconds.)

But all those inspirational quotes and pictures of kittens and bunnies on your Facebook Page Timeline won't do you much good if there are no eyeballs to see 'em.

Like a junior high school dance where students

are too scared to be the first one on the dance floor, sometimes you've got to scrape and claw your way to your first 1000 fans — so the rest of the universe thinks your page is worth "liking" and "interacting" with.

So, here are my seven favorite (mostly free) techniques to boost your fan base overnight and make your brand look way more popular than it is:

Super-Quick Fan Strategy No. 1: Leave a "Follow Us On Facebook" Suggestion Everywhere

And when I say everywhere, I mean everywhere. This could include areas such as:

- Email signature
- Forum or message board profile
- Your other social network profiles (such as Twitter, YouTube, Pinterest.)
- At the end of every blog post your

write (whether on your site or on somebody else's site)

- In the description of every YouTube video you upload
- Your brick-and mortar store's front counter
- Employee t-shirts
- Any direct mail or offline promo materials
- Media Buys, such as TV, radio, print, or online

And how do you get people to follow you? Could be something as simple as using verbiage that ties into their self-interest. Such as:

- "Follow Us on Facebook for Special Offers"
- "Like Us on Facebook for Members-Only Content"
- "Like us on Facebook for Members-Only Coupons"

Ya gotta give people an incentive, other than it would really help your teetering self-esteem. If you do, you'll see your fan count — and overall self-worth — rise in no time.

Super-Quick Fan Strategy No. 2: Put Facebook Icons on Your Blog or Website

This one SHOULD be a no-brainer, right? I mean, it's your website. (So why wouldn't you have "Like Us on Facebook" stuff there.) But many marketers still neglect to do this. (And if they do it, it's usually not done well.)

I think it's because Facebook makes the entire "liking" experience so damn confusing. People can "like" your blog post, but not necessarily "like" your Page.

They can "like" a comment, but not "like" the blog post itself. (Only Mark Zuckerberg could make me "hate" the word "like" so very much.)

Here's what you got to know…there are two prominent areas on your website or blog that you want to have Facebook icon placement:

Placement #1 - A Facebook "Like" box on the sidebar of your website.

These are those cool-looking square boxes visitors that not only show how many fans you have — and how many of those fans are their own friend — but gives visitors a chance to "like" your page without leaving your website.

This is, by far the most effective way to get new fans from visitors who frequent your website. (It's like you're getting two leads for the price of one.)

To install this like box, just head over to the Facebook Like Box Developer Page. (PunkRockMarketing.com/likebox) (They've got some, surprisingly, straightforward documentation there to help.)

You basically just:

- Create the like box plugin on the Facebook developer page.

- Insert the code into the sidebar of your website. If you're using WordPress there are plugins that specifically do this. Otherwise you can find a developer-for-hire on Fiverr.com to help.

Placement #2 - Add Facebook Comments to Your Blog Posts and/or Web Articles

Want immediate and instant feedback to the stuff you publish on your website? (I know. Scary, right?)

Don't worry, the possible downside to hearing brutal feedback from your visitors is outweighed by the awesomeness of having comments on your website, show up in your visitors' — and their friends' — newsfeed. (Talk about viral.)

Just another in a long line of reasons to ensure your website content has killer titles that catch the attention of people who have no idea who you are.

To add comments to your site, just check out the Facebook Developers Comments page for instructions on how to do it.

(http://punkrockmarketing.com/commentsbox)

Super-Quick Fan Strategy No. 3: Beg Your Friends to Like Your Page

This one may sound pathetic. (And it is.) But it works.

Considering the average Facebook user has an average of 240 friends, asking your existing (personal) Facebook network to "like" your page can be the quickest way to boost that fan total, especially for a brand-new page.

What I usually do is make an appeal that's both whimsical and self-deprecating:

"Hey guys!

"I created this awesome, amazing new Facebook Page that will completely revolutionize the entire world, and quite possibly save civilization. Unfortunately, we've only got three fans so far. (One of them is my mother.)

"Will you help us out by clicking 'like' and becoming a

fan? A grateful nation thanks you."

Feel free to leave out the "mother" part. Otherwise, the rest works well.

Super-Quick Fan Strategy No. 4: Ask Your Social Media Fans/Followers to "Like" Your Page

This is a super-easy, but often under-utilized, method for getting fans (many of whom already know you.)

And that is by asking your tribes on other social media platforms to "like your page" — or better yet respond to one of your Facebook page posts.

This includes platforms such as Twitter, Instagram, Pinterest, Tumblr…almost any you can think of. (In my experience, Twitter and Instagram are perfect for this. I wouldn't recommend Google+ however…don't want to piss off the Google gods.)

As we mentioned before, this works best if you "tease" the request to "like" your page — such as

"Follow us on Facebook to get a 10% off coupon" — or link to exciting content you've placed on your Facebook page. (I love to use surveys and quizzes in this way.)

Super-Quick Fan Strategy No.5: Put a "Follow Us" Link on Your Thank You Pages

Once somebody has bought something from you, or has opted into your email list, they are what you might refer to as a "hot lead."

So why not add them to your Facebook tribe at the same time? (And possibly keep selling to them in different ways repeatedly.)

To add some "Follow Us" code, just head over to the Facebook Developer Follow Button page (PunkRockMarketing.com/followbutton), and put in your website info and drop the code into your website.

Super-Quick Fan Strategy No. 6: Run a Contest

We're gonna go over contests in a lot more detail in Chapter 10. Just know when it comes to getting fans — FAST! — nothing beats a good, old Facebook contest.

The trouble with Facebook contests is they tend to lead to freebie-seekers — and not folks who necessarily translate to actual customers. (These are people who like to win "free crap.")

But when it comes to boosting your fan counts, Facebook contest absolutely rock.

Contests are a bit involved, technically, so head on over to Chapter 10 for more of a deep-dive on the topic.

Super-Quick Fan Strategy No. 7: Run a "Like Page" Ad

Okay, so maybe this is more of an advanced

strategy. (Mostly because it requires hard-earned moolah.)

And if you're able to get 1,000 fans using the methods above, I encourage you to do so. (Even if it means forcing all your nieces and nephews to act as unpaid social media assistants.)

But if you're STILL not able to get much traction with your Page in the "fans" department, then it might be time to invest in a "Like ad" campaign.

Here's what you should know about "Page Like" ads in the Facebook ecosystem:

- **Facebook "like ads" do one thing, invite people to "like" your page**. Don't expect them to link out to your sales page or deliver you an email subscriber.

- **They are stupidly expensive.** Especially considering what they give you. ("Like ads can run anywhere from $1-$2/like.)

- **They boost the performance of other types of Facebook ads.** We're gonna cover ads in far more depth in later chapters, but just know that having an ongoing "like ad" can really help the performance of your more targeted types of ads. (Not fair, but 'tis the way it is.)

- **You can see results by spending as little as $1/day.** You don't need to spend a ton on these. Even $1/day for just a couple of days will help the popularity of your page.

So, how do you set these types of ads up? Su-per simple!

1. Head over to your Fan page. Click on the link that says "Promote your page"

2. Select your page. (If you have more than one page.)

3. Put in a headline. I like to sell the

benefits of the page for headlines. (Whether it be special offers or insider tips.)

4.   Choose a placement. Start off with mobile and right column placements. (Desktops get way too expensive for "like ads.")

5.   Choose fans of pages that are like yours. (Go for an audience at least 2-3 million in size.)

6.   Set up your daily budget. I like to do about $1-$2 a day.

7.   And let the "like ad" do its thing.

Again these "like ad" campaigns aren't gonna put instant money in your pocket. (Sorry this isn't Forex trading or multi-level marketing.)

But it is part of an overall strategy of boosting the popularity — and more importantly the "perceived" popularity — of your page. Which will come in handy, in the next chapter.

Chapter Four Key Takeaways:

- **Place a "Follow Me on Facebook" link in any online — and offline — place you can think of.** That includes email signatures, online profiles, business cards, print ads, and in-store merch. (Just make sure to give 'em a reason to follow you — such as free stuff!)

- **Put Facebook icons on your website and/or blog to boost your fan count.** This includes a sidebar "like box" and a "comments box" to your blog posts. Don't worry about the "feedback," it'll be worth it.

- **Beg your friends to like your Fan Page.** Plead shamelessly, if required.

- **Reach out to your fans and**

followers on other social media profiles and ask them to "like" your page. (Better yet ask them for their feedback on hot-button topics.)

- **Use your Fan Page to like and comment** on other Pages. (But in a non-spammy, human way.)

- **Create a "Follow Us" link on your thank you pages.** (Nearly 50% of all people who opt-in to your email list will "like" your page, if you give them a reason.)

- **Run a simple Facebook "like" contest to increase your fan count...FAST!** (Just don't expect a ton of these new fans to turn into instant customers.)

- **Use "Click Like" ads to boost your fan base.** Even as little as a $1/day for a couple of days could do the trick. Super helpful when running more conversion-focused ads.

Chapter 5:
The How, What, When and Where of Facebook Posting

"Our chief want is someone who will inspire us to be what we know we could be."

-Ralph Waldo Emerson

Here's where we dig into the trenches of Facebook Marketing. Where we answer such eternal questions as…

- What the hell am I going to post on my Facebook Page?
- When is the best TIME to post?
- How do we attract the largest

- audience possible with our posts? (I.e.: Get fans to share stuff for us because we're too lazy to do it ourselves.)

- How do I make sure I don't waste my time with all this posting crap?

And all the tips I'm going to share in this chapter have been tested and refined the hard way. (Meaning I tried a bunch of other crap that didn't work, until I accidentally hit up on stuff that did work.)

Here's what I want you to know upfront: just because you post something doesn't mean ANYBODY is gonna see it.

Sorry, but it's true.

Since Facebook's recent Machiavellian updates…err…algorithmic changes, LESS of our stuff gets seen by OUR fans, unless we spend money "boosting" our posts.

Which means it's all about QUALITY posts, less often, over a QUANTITY of posts in the hopes that "something" catches the attention of fans.

So, now we got the bad news out of the way, let's jump right into the dos and don'ts of Facebook posting with my Facebook Publishing FAQ:

Facebook Posting FAQ #1: How Often Should You Post?

If this were five years ago, I'd have said you should post to your Fan Page EVERY day. (Maybe even 2x a day.) And if your business creates a ton of timely content, such as an online magazine, then this frequency count will still work for you.

But these days I'd say 2-3x a week is optimal — and way less time-consuming than the old "gotta post 3x a day" mandate all the gurus recommend.

You can post way more than that. But try your best to get at least 2-3 good status updates a week. (And if NOBODY is responding to any of your posts, then just hit a "boost post" to any of your updates and that'll help get your stuff noticed.)

Facebook Posting FAQ #2: What Times of the Week Should You Post?

This might be the most contentious topic in the seedy, underground world of social media guru-ness. I wish I could tell you there was absolute agreement on this subject. (But getting people to agree on a brand of coffee, let alone ideal Facebook posting times, is nearly impossible.)

But let me share with you what I've learned, having done this in a few businesses (and worked with clients to find their ideal posting time):

- Best days to post are Thursday and Friday (and to a lesser extent, Saturday)
- Worst days to post are Monday & Tuesday (more hectic the work schedule, the less Facebook-ing there is)
- 3-7pm EST is ideal for weekday posting

- 9am-12pm EST is ideal for weekend posting

Now the usual disclaimers about "this will depend greatly on your individual business" …blah, blah, blah…apply here.

But if it were me, I would focus my prime Facebook marketing energies on the period between Thursday - Saturday.

And let the rest of the business schmucks waste breath trying to fill their Facebook page with content every day.

Facebook Posting FAQ #3: What Kind of Stuff Should You Post?

In Chapter 1, I went over some ways to generate content for your Facebook page posts. (Such as blog posts, videos, motivational quotes.) And you can do your own testing to find a weekly content quota that works for you.

But let me give you a rough weekly breakdown

of the kinds of stuff I like to share on my Facebook page — and on which days I like to feature them:

Week One

- Thursday - Blog post (created in-house)
- Friday - Motivational Quote
- Saturday - Hot-Button (Fill-in-the-Blank) Question

Week Two

- Thursday - Video me (created in-house)
- Friday - Funny video
- Saturday - Hot-Button (Fill-in-the-Blank) Question

Week Three

- Thursday - Infographic or blog post (created in-house)
- Friday - Motivational Quote
- Saturday - Hot-Button (Fill-in-the-

Blank) Question

Week Four

- Thursday - Video pitching something or promoting something for sale
- Friday - Motivational Quote
- Saturday - Hot-Button (Fill-in-the-Blank) Question

Couple things you might have gathered from this weekly breakdown:

- **The only thing I share on Friday is "motivational" quote**s. That's because human brains have Kardashian-level potential on Fridays. (So, all ya wanna do is give 'em something to silly to look at.)
- **Thursdays are where I focus my in-house content and special offers.** This is where I find my

most captive — and lucrative — Facebook fan audience.

- **Saturdays are great for engagement with posts that don't require a lot of time.** I don't recommend you ask your fans to read your 12K-word blog post on a Saturday, but having people answer a survey or check out some other fun, visual piece of content is wholly acceptable.

- **I only "promote or sell" something once a month.** That's because my stuff is on the higher-ticket range. You may want to promote lower-ticket items (more often).

- **I promote with a video.** In Chapter 8, I'm gonna walk you through exactly how to use video to create devastatingly effective ads.

But for now, just know if yer selling "anything" that requires more than a $20 investment, it's helpful to have a video that "pre-sells" the product or service. (Doesn't have to be long, just something that educates them about why they need the product or service RIGHT this frickin' moment.)

Facebook Posting FAQ #4: How Do I Actually Post Something on Facebook?

So, once you've got your posting schedule nailed down — and have a rough idea of the kinds of things you'll be sharing on your Facebook page — it's time to get that stuff published for public consumption.

Here's my eight keys to the perfect Facebook post:

1. **Try your best to "schedule" and**

"publish" your posts through the Facebook platform. I know there are plenty of third-party tools, such as HootSuite and Post Planner, that let you handle all your Facebook publishing. But evidence suggests Facebook "penalizes" content published through these tools.

2. **Always attach a photo to your post** — unless it's a video. And if yer promoting content that lives outside Facebook, try to use the same photo found on that landing page.

3. **Ideal Facebook photo size for your posts is 1200x630 pixels**. This will be probably change by the time I finish typing this sentence but aim for this size for now.

4. **Keep your Facebook posts less than 80 characters if possible**. Turns out posts under 80 characters get 23% more

interaction. Which might be easier to explain when you realize 75% of all Facebook posts are longer than 80 characters. (You'll stand out!)

5.   **Use brackets to categorize your post.** For example, you could do something like: [blog] or [video] or [question of the week] or [quote]. This not only provides a shorthand for Facebook users to understand what yer pitching, but the special characters also stand out in a sea of content.

6.   **Pick your posts when asking people "What do you think?"** There was a time when I suggested folks asked "What do you think? Let us know in the comments below" in every single post. But that's passé these days. (And takes up valuable real estate.) So, be judicious about asking for feedback. (Don't worry they'll give it.)

7. **If you're promoting a good cause, ask people to "like" and "share" your post.** Back in the olden days of 2011, you could ask folks to "like" every single thing you put out there. (But now it's seen as obnoxious.) Unless you're promoting something on the charitable end of things. Then knock yourself out.

8. **Super-sneaky trick:** once you publish your post click on the "date stamp" and this will bring up a URL of your individual post. With this URL you can promote your individual page posts in places like Twitter, Pinterest, Instagram, LinkedIn…or wherever else you can think of!

Chapter Five Key Takeaways:

- **Ya don't need to post every day.** In fact, 2-3x a week seems like a good weekly posting mix for Facebook.

- **Best days to post are Thursday and Friday.** (With 3-7pm EST being the Facebook post sweet spot.)

- **You can post whatever you want…but I like to share quotes** (especially on Fridays), blog posts, videos, and the occasional promotion. (No more than 1x a month.)

- **Posting your content on Facebook is dead easy.** Try to keep your post text under 80 characters, use bracket descriptors, and aim for a photo size of 1200x630.

Chapter 6:
Creating a Facebook Ad Strategy That Doesn't Suck (and Actually Makes You Money)

"It's not the impression you make, it's the impression you leave."

-Marilyn Schwartz

Ah, yes…Facebook ads. The scourge and bane of most every small-business owner who's dipped their toes into the pool of Facebook marketing.

Trust me: I know how FRUSTRATING running

Facebook ad campaigns can be.

And if you've tried Facebook ads in the past, with inconsistent results, just know, it's not your FAULT. (The system is pretty much set up for you to fail.)

That's because:

- Facebook likes to change the "look" and "feel" of its ad platform every 12 seconds

- Facebook "might" have the most user-unfriendly ad dashboard ever created (and I've used the Bing ad platform!)

- Facebook is notoriously picky about which ads they will — or won't — allow

- …most important of all, Facebook users HATE clicking on ANYTHING that has the appearance of marketing

And if Facebook didn't hold the key to the most targeted, focused leads our business could ever find…

…then I'd say you can tell those Silicon Valley Millennials to take their $1.32/like ads and shove it up their newsfeed.

But, alas, Facebook ads DO represent an under-utilized and super-ninja way to find a swath of new leads and long-term customers.

And once you figure out how to get some successful Facebook ad campaigns running on auto-pilot — and over the next few chapters I'm going to show you how to do just that — not only will you be making a crap load more money…

…but you'll also chuckle to yourself as the competition complains about how "hard" Facebook ads are to run. ("Let them eat cake…and their crappy Facebook ads.")

So, if you're READY to begin your quest for world domination, let's jump right in with my 4 Keys to Profitable Facebook Ads:

Profitable Facebook Ads Key #1: Keep Your Eye on the Big Picture

Having spent enough money on Facebook ads to buy my first car, a 1983 Honda Civic, SEVEN times over…

…I can tell you the NUMBER ONE reason most Facebook ads fail is not targeting or bid strategy or bad copywriting (though all of that can certainly derail even the best ad)…

…it's unrealistic expectations.

We create Facebook ads like we do any other piece of paid media. We design ads that tout our latest offering and serve it in front of eyeballs we think SHOULD be interested…and wait for the cash register to start cha-ching.

And when it doesn't, we consider ourselves, or the entire Facebook ad platform, a total failure.

But that's because we're expecting a tiny little ad — which most people will see while scrolling on their smart phone on the toilet — to do all this sales heavy-lifting for us.

When what we need to do is understand the Facebook ad long game. And that "long game" is:

- **Step #1: Introduce Yourself to "Cold" Prospects (With a Content Ad)** — In which you share your best content — your most passionate, kick-ass stuff — with your ideal target audience. (And sneakily add that website visitor to your "retargeting" contact list.)

- **Step #2: Offer Your Freebie to "Warm" Prospects (With a Pre-Sell Video Ad**) — In which you create a video that tells people, who've ALREADY consumed your stuff, what your freebie is about (and why they desperately need it.)

- **Step #3: Offer Your Freebie Again (Nicely) to "Warm"**

Prospects Who Haven't Opted In yet (With Facebook Retargeting Ads) — In which we create super-sneaky retargeting ads that "follow" our would-be leads throughout the Facebook universe.

Now each of these ad steps are super important — and require some precision to make work — so we're gonna break 'em up into the next three chapters. But for now, just digest this: no SINGLE Facebook ad lives in isolation. (They all work together to create a wonderful symphony of marketing awesomeness.)

Because approaching Facebook ads lets you:

- Get past a Facebook user's usual resistance to clicking on ads
- Disguise sales pitches as actual content (Totally ninja)
- Squeeze MORE profit out of every single drop of website traffic (the

part I really love)

So, no matter what Facebook ad "hangover" you may have — give this method a try. You'll be surprised how profitable — and less stressful — this strategy can be.

Facebook Ad Key #2: Sync Your Account With Facebook Business Manager

Before you freak out I'm asking you to sign up for ANOTHER weird social media contraption, just know Facebook business manager is:

- A great tool for keeping all your Facebook page and ad activity in one centralized hub (away from your personal stuff)
- The perfect way to manage numerous Facebook pages (and multiple admins) without wires

getting crossed

- Likely to be the only way in the future for you to access more advanced Facebook marketing features (such as Power Editor and Ads Manager)

To sign up all you gotta do is head over to business.facebook.com and sign in with your current account and follow the steps to migrate your account over to a business account.

And though you could certainly avoid this step — if you prefer to keep your existence as Zuckerberg-free as possible — I heartily recommend you make the big leap over to Business Facebook Manager. (If only so you won't have to create ads with that annoying "Dodger blue" color scheme staring back at you.)

Facebook Ad Key #3: Get That All-Important Targeting Code Set Up

We went over this in Chapter 2, but this is a good time to double-check you've got that all-important Facebook retargeting code set up on every page on your website. (That includes landing pages and thank you pages that live on other platforms, such as LeadPages.)

Trust me: you want to do this as soon as possible. (Otherwise you're leaving money on the Facebook advertising table.) And if you're unsure HOW to do this, find a degenerate developer on Fiverr or Upwork do it for you.

Bonus Tip: While you're at it, pasting code all over your virtual kingdom, you might as well get your Google Analytics and Google Retargeting code in there as well. (It's better to have too much data, rather than not enough.)

Facebook Ad Key #4: Have Your Marketing Funnel as Bullet-Proof as Possible

Marketing funnels evolve over time. (So, you don't have to make sure it's perfect before jumping into the world of Facebook ads.)

But right before you set up your first campaign take one last tour through your funnel. (Or better yet have a total stranger do it.)

You want to make sure the messaging (and the user experience) is exactly how you want it in areas such as:

- Your freebie giveaway
- Your landing page
- Your email follow-up sequence (if you have one)
- Your sales pages
- Your upsell pages (and downsell pages) — if you got 'em

- The look and feel of your Facebook page
- Your website (especially those "About Us" and "Contact Us" pages, which I find interminably boring, but users actually do check it out)

Does the copy and imagery on all these different touch points deliver on your CORE MESSAGE? (Do you have a core message?)

Do these different tentacles of your marketing octopus do a great job of: Presenting a compelling offer AND Converting on that offer.

If not, rewrite it. Or re-design it. Or cut it out of the funnel.

But if you feel you've got your funnel dialed in, then you ready for one of the coolest, most ninja ways to use Facebook — promote your kick-ass marketing (disguised as content.)

Chapter Six Key Takeaways:

- **The #1 key to Facebook advertising success is to remember it's a long-term gain with THREE key components** — 1) Introducing yourself with content ads 2) which you follow up with pre-sell videos that tout your freebie 3) then follow up with retargeting ads that (gently) nudge people to sign up for your email list.

- **Facebook Business Manager isn't just an obnoxious term for Silicon Valley world domination.** It's a convenient tool to manage all your Facebook marketing activities — and gives you access to the shiny toys Facebook provides marketers, such as Power Editor.

- **Set up that Facebook retargeting**

code before running your ads. The Author really encourages you not to be dumb like he did and wait six months before doing this.

- **Do a test-run through your entire marketing funnel before running your ads.** The Author also strongly encourages this as he wishes he had a time machine and had done this before spending thousands of dollars on Facebook ads.

Chapter 7:

How to Use Content Ads to Boost Your Brand (and Bottom Line)

*"Nobody reads ads. They read what interests them.
Sometimes they happen to be ads."*
-Howard Luck Gossage

I know you're gonna have resistance to running these kinds of ads. And trust me, I get it. I HATE running any kind of ad, especially on shallow social media platforms, that don't IMMEDIATELY put money in my pocket.

But here's the thing about Facebook: Nobody, not even your most die-hard, stalkerish fans open their Facebook app on their smartphone so they can learn how to get 50% off your Google Adwords course or discover how they can take advantage of your limited-time dental marketing coaching plan.

They go to Facebook to comment on pictures of their friends' kids — or watch videos of pugs dressed up like "Yoda." They DON'T want to make decisions or spend money or do anything.

There's a reason Facebook is called the "modern smoke break." People use it to "turn off" their brain — not discover how you can help them consolidate their student loan.

But if you're somehow able to cut through the noise and offer them a shortcut or ninja-hack strategy or crazy funny video that speaks to the situation they're in at that moment — and I'll show you how to do just that — you will move into a different part of their brain.

The part of their brain they reserve for cool, funny people they "like" and "trust."

And there's no quicker route to that part of their cerebral cortex than a good, old piece of kick-ass content. (Supported by a content ad or two to make sure it gets seen by the eyeballs of your future customers.)

Facebook Content Ad Step #1: Have Your Killer Piece of Content Ready to Go

We went over this in Chapter 2 in some detail — check back there if you need a refresher course — but the key here is to have a signature piece of content that shares your message and genuinely helps improve the lives of people who check it out.

What kind of content should you share? Well, that'll depend on your audience. If you're trying to reach lawyers, that 60-second Instagram selfie video you shot standing in front of your bathroom mirror probably isn't a good fit.

And if you're looking to connect with "World of Warcraft" fans, then a 2000-word article on LinkedIn will do nuthin' for ya.

But, really, it comes down to this question:

What piece of content (and more importantly what form of content) can I create that will get people to stop scrolling through their smart phone and check out my stuff?

In my experience "list-type" blog posts — such as "5 Things Every CEO Can Learn From Ozzy Osbourne" — or benefit-rich videos work well. ("My #1 Secret to Creating a Viral Video (Without a Camera or Anything to Say.")

Though may need to test which works better for your audience, text-driven content or visual-driven content.

For my niche businesses catering to writers — they prefer the written word above video. But for my business catering to realtors, they'd rather have an icepick to the brain then read anything over 500 words.

Just know you want to make this your BEST stuff. Your super dazzling piece of amazing-ness that causes rioting in the streets — and brings a revolution to your industry. (Or at least to the minds of your potential customers.)

Facebook Content Ad Step #2: Know the Facebook Ad Lingo

So, there's a Facebook elephant in the room I'm having to deal with before we can move forward. And that's the confusion surrounding two similarly named types of Facebook content ads: boosted posts and page posts.

I know this is confusing because it took me months to get these straight. (I'm certain Mark Zuckerberg did this intentionally to make me feel dumb.)

But here's what you need to know:

- A **"boosted post"** is where you

create a usual, run-of-the-mill status update on your Facebook page where you include a link to your piece of content — but as a bonus you choose the "boost post" option. For just a few dollars you can get your post seen by many your fans and followers. (Simplest type of content ad to run.)

- A **"page post"** is where you create an ad in your Facebook ads manager — not directly in your Facebook page platform — and create a special Facebook post that allows you more text and better targeting options. (More complex, but you can get your ad in front of targeted eyeballs.)

How do you KNOW which type of content ad to run? I'm so glad you asked…

Facebook Content Ad Step #3: Make a Content Ad Plan

Here's what I like to do for each of my pieces of KILLER CONTENT:

- **Phase #1: Share that content on my Facebook Page as a status update** — and then "boost" that content to my existing fans. I'll usually spend $10-$15 over the course of a couple days to do this. Just helps prime the pump — not to mention get some much-needed engagement going on my page.

- **Phase #2: After the "boost post" campaign is done, I'll create a "page post" campaign** in my Ads Manager. I generally like to start with a small daily bid for this type of ad — about $5 or so — and give it three days. (If it ain't getting at least a 3-5% click rate — or view rate, for video — then I'll tweak the ad. Or try another piece of content.)

And that's the plan. Su-per simple. And once ya got that, it's time to put together the creative assets for your content ad…

Facebook Content Ad Step #4: Create a Compelling Picture (For Text-Based Content)

If yer gonna share a video, don't worry about this step. (Your video will dynamically generate a thumbnail for ya when you create a Facebook content ad from it.) But if you're sharing any kind of written content, you'll want a compelling image to grab people's attention.

And though I am the world's worst graphic designer — and the world's second-worst photographer — here are a couple guidelines I've picked up when procuring that all-important

Facebook content ad picture:

- **Ideal size for your picture is 1200x628**. Though this could change by the time I finish this sentence. Until then, opt for a picture in this ratio.

- **Faces looking directly at the camera**, or strong abstract visuals always work well. Your job is not to be subtle, it is to be seen.

- **Black and white pictures stand out well**. Especially in a sea of other Facebook posts. Try it out, you might be surprised.

- **Use colors that contrast nicely with the BLUE Facebook color scheme**. Oranges, reds, and yellows work well. Blues and purples, not so much.

- **Insert a text overlay at the TOP that bears the "title" of your**

piece of content. Ya can't assume people are gonna read the copy of your post. Let the image do the talking — and that talking should include "Here's the awesome cool thing this content is about. (And put it at the top, or middle, so it doesn't get cut off at the bottom.)

- **Make sure text doesn't take up more than 20% of the overall image.** This is an iron-clad Facebook rule, if you violate it they will reject your ad.

- **Create 2-3 different images for each piece of content.** I know this is a pain and a little bit of extra work, but you'll be surprised how different images can lead to very different results.

And once ya got your photo set up, it's time for…

Facebook Content Ad Key #5: Write That Killer Ad Copy

Because there are essentially two kinds of content ads — the initial "boost post" ad and the "page post" ad — there are two bits of ad copy ya gotta create. (But don't worry I've got templates for both that you can follow.)

Here's how I like to organize my "boost posts"....

Bracket Descriptor + Juicy Benefit-Laden Headline (Along with a reminder how this benefit is way easier to achieve than people think)

Examples would be:

[blog] 5 reasons why carrier pigeon messages will become the new social network (and how to master it in 5.3 seconds)

[video] My 3 best webinar marketing strategies — and none of them take longer than five minutes

Remember these are all about: Killer results WITHOUT pain, time, or effort. (Skip the fancy copywriting books and focus on that.)

For the "Page Post" copy, we get more text to work with. There are three areas we need to focus on: The Text, Headline and News Feed Link Description.

Here's how I break them down:

- **Text** - this is the big block of text at the top. (ABOVE the headline…I know. Weird, right?) And this is where I like to include a) who I'm talking to b) what benefit my piece of content will offer 'em and c) who I am and why they should listen.

Example: "Hey Screenwriter! Curious what legendary filmmaker Buster Keaton can teach you about writing for the screen? Find out in this new column from your screenwriting Sherpa, Michael Rogan, of ScriptBully Magazine."

- **Headline** - Again, the headline is BELOW the description. (Boggles the mind.) But this is simple. Just use a bracket descriptor and a title headline for the piece of content. (Not unlike what you used in the "boost post" copy.

Example: "[blog] 5 Hacks Every Screenwriter Should STEAL From Buster Keaton"

- **News Feed Link Description** - This is the piece of text at the very bottom. And this is an area most marketers screw up — because they think this is ABOUT "selling" the content. Instead they should see this as an area of "previewing" the content. Just jump right in and give 'em a quick slice of what you're gonna do. (Add a "No.1" if you can. Makes it sound more official.)

Example: "Screenwriting Hack #1: The More Serious Your Characters Are, the Funnier They'll Be..."

And when you've got your status update copy nailed down, for both the "boosted post" and the "Page post" you'll be ready for the final step…

Facebook Content Ad Key #5: Upload That Sucker

This is the easiest part of the whole system. Don't believe me? Just watch:

- **Step #1 - Share your content as a status update and simply click "boost post."** Depending on the # of fans you have, plan on spending $10-$20 over the course of a few days. (You don't need total saturation, just some likes and comments.) Note: Don't target "friends of fans" unless you feel they are part of your ideal demographic. (For instance, if you were running a local business.)

- **Step #2 - Create a "Page Post" ad**, when your "boost post" promotion has run its course. Give it at least 3 days before ditching the Page post.

Now the actual process for creating these types of ads seems to change weekly — so I recommend you check out the documentation that Facebook creates for these types of ads. You can access that by heading over to PunkRockMarketing.com/PagePost.

But a few things to keep in mind:

- **Choose "Video Views" or "Clicks to website" as your campaign objective.** Don't worry about conversions.

- **You want to create what's called a "dark post."** This just means you'll create an ad that won't be published to your page. (Ya don't need it. You already covered that with your "boosted post.")

- **Try "Desktop" and "Desktop Right Column" as ad placements first.** And then add "Mobile" or "Instagram" if you're getting good performance from the ad.

- **For "suggested bid" choose an amount .10 over the minimum range suggested.** You can always lower it later…ya just want to give your ad a chance out of the gate.

- **You want to target "Fans" of your competitor's pages** — or fans of pages that are in a similar industry as yours. (For example, if I was a golf shop then I'd target fans of golf magazines, golf blogs, golf manufacturers…in addition to other local golf shops.)

- **Specify you want your ad to show only in the U.S., Canada, U.K. and Australia.** Unless, of course, your business caters to non-English-speaking countries.

- **Feel free to use a "tracking link" in the ad under website URL.** (Google Analytics is perfect for this.)

- **Start with a small daily ad spend limit — about $5 or so.** And then work your way up from there. (You want to see results before you invest more.)

- **Have a target audience of at least 500K- 1 million folks before you run your ad.** Any less than that and you might not be reaching anybody.

- **If you're sharing a video, upload that video straight to the Facebook ads manager.** Don't just share a YouTube video. (You'll get better results if you upload the video straight to your Fan Page.)

- **Don't get too hung up on instant conversions.** You want clicks and video views. (Don't forget if you've got your retargeting set up properly, then you're collecting them as a lead already.)

Chapter Seven Key Takeaways:

- **The biggest key to Facebook content ad success is…well…killer content.** The type of content you present will depend on your market. (But list-type blog posts and "my #1 strategy" videos work well.)

- **There are two kinds of Facebook ads — they have annoyingly similar names.** They are "boosted posts" — which are simply status updates that are "boosted" and "page posts" which are Facebook ads that promote content to very targeted audiences.

- **The ideal Facebook content plan** "usually" includes 2-3 days of "boosting" a post, and then 3-5 more days of a targeted "page post."

- **If you're going to promote a text-based piece of content, then you'll need a killer picture to promote that content.** Key features of this killer photo include standout colors (no blues or purples), final photo size of 1200x628, and a text overlay that contains the title of your piece of content.

- **Write your ad copy BEFORE you head over to the Facebook ads manager.** Sell benefits of the content — as well as a brief reminder why they should listen to you. (Bonus ninja tip: Use the News Feed Link Description field in your page post to "preview" your content. Nobody else does this.)

- **Uploading your ad (finally) is**

relatively easy. (Even if the process changes every week.) Don't forget to: choose "video views" or "website click" as your goal, find fans of competitor (or industry) pages, gather an audience at least 500K-1 Million in size, and start your bidding off low (about $5/day) and raise slowly up from there.

Chapter 8:

How to Get Super-Cheap Leads With Facebook Video Ads

"The absolute aim should be to make money out of satisfying customers."
-John Egan

Finally! We're going to, at long last, get to the MEAT of this whole Facebook ad strategy…and that is get some actual frickin' leads into our marketing funnel.

Now, you can go straight to this ad type — and

skip the whole content ad step — if you really, really want to.

But I don't recommend it.

Having gone through this dog-and-pony show quite a few times I can confidently assert if you introduce yourself using content ads FIRST, before you go for the Facebook marketing kill, you will be rewarded with:

- Lower ad costs
- Higher click thru rates
- Higher conversion rates
- Lower refund rates
- More long-term customers

And the reason is simple: by introducing yourself first (and offering value first) you'll lower folks' resistance to your message. (And put them in a state where they're ready for your Jedi marketing tricks.)

Okay, enough of the pedantic lecture. Let me walk you through my 5-step Facebook Pre-Sell Video Ad Process:

Pre-Sell Video Ad Step #1: Figure Out What Yer Gonna Say

I know you're champing at the bit to get in front of that camera and riff away about your wonderful, dynamic, earth-changing video.

But here's what you gotta remember:

- People get bored and distracted easily (So if you don't grab their attention, you're toast)
- People don't want to say "yes" to you (Which is why you've got to make it imperative they act)
- People are always wondering WHO the hell is this guy or girl talking to me?

Now we went over this pre-sell video structure in some detail So, before you begin riffing away, I recommend you follow this simple, but effective Pre-Sell Video Ad Formula that I follow:

1. **The "Click Start"** — Start off your video by looking directly at the camera and saying, "Click to hear the video" TWICE as you point downward (near your chest). There's a reason for this, it encourages people to click on your video in their feed while on their Smartphone. This alone will boost click rates nearly 40%.

2. **Introduce yourself** — You wanna keep this brief, but it's important you tell them who you are (and why you're talking.) "Hey this is Larry Rothschild from MicroChip Remover and in this video and I want to tell you about HOW to remove that microchip from your brain the Facebook thought police implanted there…" — Note: If you have different customer segments, create different versions of this video so there's a better message to market

match.

3.   **Tell them the WHY** — Give them context for WHY it's so damn important they grab your freebie, stress urgency and pain if they don't do it — "All of us know free will is important…but did you know Mark Zuckerberg is controlling your every thought and movement from an underground bunker in Menlo Park…"

4.   **Acknowledge their obstacles** — "The trouble is, it's hard to find the time or motivation to deal with the microchip. Or even know how to get started."

5.   **Introduce your freebie** — "I think I may have found the perfect solution and it's all revealed in my FREE REPORT 'How to Remove the Facebook MicroChip from your brain….'"

6.   **Brief story about your journey** — "I first realized I had my own Facebook

micro-chip problem when I wandered through Silicon Valley, naked, asking for "my buddy Mark Z. And I said to myself: 'There has to be a better way!'"

7. **Tell 'em how to get their freebie —** "And to learn my micro-chip removal system…all you gotta do is click in this post."

8. **Wish them well —** "Hope to see ya on the other side, but in case I don't I wish you much good luck in your pursuit of being the best and micro-chip free person you can be."

Pre-Sell Video Ad Step #2: Film and Edit the Damn Thing

I know the thought of turning that camera on might induce enough anxiety to require a Lexapro prescription, but just know your video doesn't have to be PERFECT.

It doesn't even have to be in the kingdom of perfect. (In fact, in some markets, the more polished and professional your video looks, the worse it converts.)

But here are FOUR must-haves your pre-sell video needs to be successful:

1. **Good Sound** — This is a deal-breaker. You MUST have good sound. If somebody can't hear your video, if it's recorded with an external Mic that makes you sound like you're speaking from a Sears washer/dryer, nobody will ever watch your video. So, whether you film on a $2800 DSLR or your smart phone make sure you've got decent audio. (And this usually means having some kind of external microphone plugged in to your camera.)

2. **Video Performer Who Gives a Crap** — This might be you. (And probably is.) But resist the temptation many small

biz types fall prey to do to put the most "photogenic" or "attractive" person on camera. "He/She who cares most, wins…" and whoever that is in your business, makes sure they're the ones doing the communicating.

3.　**A Mix of Fast and Slow** — This is an advanced public speaker tip, but one of the best ways to really engage listeners is to vary the tempo of your message. So, when you get to the part of your video that's important…slow it down. Give it more emphasis. But you when you want to do drum up excitement, speed up. (Simple, but effective.)

4.　**Photos to "Cut Against"** — Sorry, 'bout the video jargon, but it's good to have a couple of still images (that relate to your topic) that you can "cut to" while you keep talking. We want to do this because a) It hides our mistakes (even though you and I both know you're not going to make any) and b) It breaks up the monotony of people looking at your mug. (Break up a static image every 15-20 seconds.)

And though this isn't a book about video editing — Thank God! — I do want to say video editing is like changing the oil in your car. If you enjoy doing it, knock yourself out. But if it fills you with mortal dread, just have somebody else do it.

Pre-Sell Video Ad Step #3: Upload That Sucker

Here's the fun part! Where we get to upload this piece of marketing art you've created.

Now, as I've detailed earlier, Facebook likes to "change" their ad process quite a bit. But here are guidelines to keep in mind when you create your video pre-sell ad:

- **Target people who checked out your content — such as a blog post or a video — but did NOT reach your "Thank You" page.** You do this by creating a "custom audience" that includes anybody who visited any of your website pages…but did NOT visit your "Thank You" page. By targeting people who've already encountered your brand you'll be paying next to nothing for leads.

- **You can either use the Power Editor or Business Manager to create your Video Ads.** There is talk of doing away with one if not both. But, at this moment, Power Editor gives you more options — but is harder to figure out. Ads Manager is easier to use — but has less options. (I'd recommend creating your first couple ads with Ads Manager and then easing yourself into the deep end of the Power Editor pool.)

- **Choose "Video Views" as your ad campaign objective at first.** And when you've got a bunch of data to work with, and you're getting leads, ease up to a "Conversion" objective.

- **When it comes to ad copy for a video ad, there are two components ya gotta nail:** a) The verb-filled copy to sell the benefits of the video. "Discover my #1 secret"; "Uncover the #1 Thing Google Doesn't Want you to Know…" and b) A LINK to your freebie "Get It Here==> www.microchip.com" (Note: You don't really have to "introduce yourself" the copy. The video does that.)

- **Choose "Learn More" as your "Video CTA."** You have a choice of "video CTA" text options, such as "Download." Just remember people love to learn — and hate "downloading" things.

- **Keep your bidding low — as low as $1-$2/day**. Because you're targeting folks who've already checked your content your # of video views will be low — but your cost of lead acquisition will be super low. (When you see gains, slowly move that bid amount up.)

Pre-Sell Video Ad Step #4: Slowly Broaden Your Video Ad's Reach

Here's where things get really ninja.

Once you've got a video pre-sell ad that's working for you — that's bringing in leads at an acquisition cost you're comfortable with — it's time to broaden that video out to the bigger Facebook world.

Not just folks who've already checked out your content in the past.

I highly recommend you wait to roll this type of video ad until you're sure you've got a winner on your hands. (And by winner, I mean something that's making money.)

But once you've got a video that's resonating with your ideal customer demographic, feel free to SKIP the whole content ad process and see how your video does with a much-larger Facebook target audience.

The process for publishing these ads is nearly the same as we just outlined in Step #3, with just a couple of tweaks:

- **Start with "Video Views" as the**

objective. After a week, change it to "conversion." (Using your "Thank You" page as the destination.)

- **Start with a daily bid that's higher than the earlier video ads, somewhere in the $10-$15 range.** (At least for the first day.) The reason for this is, if you're able to get 1000 video views in that first day — and with video view costs hovering around .01-.02 per it's totally doable — Facebook will create a "custom audience" based on people who watched your view. (This means you can present these folks offers at a future date, even if they watch your video and NEVER opt-in to your email list.)

- **Experiment with segmenting your target audience further and**

further until you can't improve your ad's performance anymore. This is the real secret sauce to your Facebook ads. To keep refining your target audience, slowly and steadily, until it's so awesome you're practically printing money from Facebook ads.

And what we've gone over so far will not only get you a Ph.D. in Facebook Ad Studies but will also help you crush (in a nice way) the competition…and literally get 200-300% more profit from your existing ad spend.

But it's in the next chapter where we're gonna go over my favorite absolute sneaky, clandestine — and super-powerful — form of online marketing going these days.

And it's a strategy that can not only help you sell a crap load of your stuff to new customers — at bargain-basement ad prices — but help you encourage those pesky non-buying past customers of yours reach for their wallets, again and again.

Chapter Eight Key Takeaways:

- **Before you film your pre-sell video, take time to map out what you will say.** Follow the system I outlined earlier, paying attention to the story you're telling, and the pain points you're hitting. (Don't sell…tell!)

- **When it comes to "performing" your video, just remember good audio is always more important than good video.** (And put the person MOST passionate about the subject — not the most photogenic — on camera.)

- **And as for editing: if you enjoy it, do it.** If you don't, have somebody else do it.

- **Setting up your video ad is easy.** (You can use either the Power

Editor or Ads Manager.) You just want to target folks who've already visited your website. (And ya need little in terms of daily ad budget, couple dollars a day will do.)

- **When you've got a pre-sell video ad that's working** — people are clicking on it and you are getting new leads — expand that video ad to target your ideal customer demographic.

Chapter 9: Facebook Retargeting Ads…The Final (Profitable) Frontier

"I find it useful to remember that everybody lives by selling something."

-Robert Louis Stevenson

This is where things get Exciting. Almost "too" exciting.

In fact, you probably shouldn't read this chapter. There's just way too much awesome ninja marketing info here.

And, for your brain's sake, you might want to close this chapter and move on to something more palatable. (Like that "alien invasion" sci-fi novel you've got in your Kindle queue.)

But…if you're looking for a way to wring every ounce of profit out of your prospects, leads, and customers then I want to introduce you to the fabulous, wonderful world of Facebook Retargeting Ads!

A Brief Primer on Retargeting

Just in case you're not up on your oddly named marketing terms — most likely because you were busy trying to run an actual business — retargeting is a process in which:

- A website visitor lands on one of your webpages
- That web page places an invisible piece of "tracking code" on that visitor's page (Through the use of harmless "cookies")
- You "follow" that user throughout

the Internet — both on Facebook or Google or wherever — by offering "targeted" ads related to the webpages they've already visited

This is how Home Depot "seems" to be reading your mind as they show you Black and Decker power drill ads as you surf the Internet. (Do people still "surf" the Internet? Does that expression make me sound old? Probably yes on both counts.)

The Cool Ninja S*#&@ You Can Do With Retargeting

Okay, now you know how it works. Here's where the mind-blowing part comes in. Because with retargeting you can do things like:

- Remarket to landing page visitors who don't opt-in
- Remarket to new email subscribers who don't buy your initial offer

- Remarket to new customers who don't take your upsell (or downsell)
- Offer existing customers different products (such as upgrades, further training, automated services)
- Re-engage existing customers who've stopped opening your emails
- Ask existing customers/subscribers to provide a testimonial, fill out a survey, leave an online review, "like" your Facebook page…do almost anything you want them to

Retargeting (or remarketing) ain't about selling stuff. It's about cutting through the distraction and clutter of modern life — and start up a one-on-one conversation with a member of your tribe.

Might be the most powerful weapon us marketers have been given since the sales letter.

But how do we get started with this powerful (though somewhat technical) marketing strategy?

Well, here are SIX key methods I'd use in your Facebook retargeting efforts:

(Note: This isn't a book about retargeting, but the strategies I outline could be used with Google retargeting, or any other retargeting platform, with relative ease.)

Cool Ninja Facebook Retargeting Method #1: Share Your Content With Email/Blog Subscribers (Easy)

This is probably the simplest retargeting method there is, and yet many marketers who produce content on a somewhat regular basis neglect to do this. And that is for just a couple bucks promote every piece of NEW content (or OLD content) to folks who haven't seen it.

Why would you want to do this?

- It boosts the SEO of your content (The more eyeballs and social shares you get, the better your content will rank)

- Gives value to your subscribers/customers (Nice deposit in the future goodwill bank)

- Gives folks who haven't opted in yet, but have read your content, a chance to "finally" join your funnel

- Most important: Helps you segment your subscriber/customer base (If I share a blog post on "Facebook marketing" and 40% of my subscribers check it out, then I can create an even more targeted future Facebook offer for just those 40%)

Now for this type of retargeting ad, I wouldn't go to the trouble of creating a video. (Think that's just overkill.) All you gotta do is:

- Create a Facebook custom audience based on your existing email subscriber list or customer list (You can do this by just uploading an Excel sheet of your contacts)

- Create a Facebook content ad (we went over these in Chapter 7)
- Target that ad to both your subscriber/customer custom audience, and target anybody who visited your website and did NOT opt-in
- Set the daily bidding for that campaign at $1-$2/day
- Sit back and watch all that delicious, new traffic to your content (and the new leads this traffic will provide)

Cool Ninja Facebook Retargeting Method #2: Get Warm (ish) Prospects to Opt-In to Your Email List (Finally!)

This one's self-explanatory. All you do is:

- Create a Facebook custom audience

compiled of ANYBODY who visited ANY page on your website — or watched one of your videos on Facebook — but did NOT land on your "Thank You" page

- Create a Facebook retargeting ad that gives them another chance to opt-in
- Set the bidding at $1/day

The real magic comes from how flexible this type of retargeting ad can be. You can:

- Share a piece of content that answers any "objections" you think they might have
- Point them to a page where you've got testimonials and social proof of people who've consumed your freebie
- Show 'em the "same" pre-sell video you created before — or send 'em

straight to the same email capture page

What you do will depend entirely on WHY people aren't opting in. (Might have nothing to do with the landing page and everything to do with the audience that's consuming it.)

But in my experience answering objections — especially about how "easy" and "simple" a solution is — and testimonials is the best way to use this form of retargeting.

Cool Ninja Facebook Retargeting Method #3: Remarket to Shopping Cart Abandoners

Everybody knows this form of retargeting. This is the "Big Brother is following you all around the Internet showing you that same DAMN Hewlett Packard printer from Costco" feeling.

The reason you see so many of these types of ads is they work. (Devastatingly well.) The trick

is to make **SURE** you balance proper follow-up with respecting people's privacy.

Here are some recommendations when creating these types of retargeting ads:

- **Limit time length these ads can be shown to 30 days.** Don't bother marketing to folks who went to your page eight months ago.

- **Cap the frequency of these ads to 15-20 times a month, per person.** Any more than that and you risk a good, old restraining order.

- **Make sure ad touts the exact product or service the would-be customer was looking for.** Don't offer them everything in your suite of products. Just show them what they were interested in.

- **Videos and/or articles that offer testimonials — and answer objections — work great.**

Especially the testimonial part, I've seen those collect as much as 50% of lost shopping cart revenue.

- **Be nice and self-deprecating.** Don't be a spammy, creepy jerk with these ads. ("I noticed you DIDN'T buy our thing!") Just present the offer in a slightly different way, with more information.

- **If people aren't buying, re-think your product's pitch**. Might be your product isn't resonating with people. (For whatever reason.) Use this type of retargeting ad as the cheapest focus group of all time.

Cool Ninja Facebook Retargeting Method #4: Offer an Upsell (or New Product) to Your Existing Customers

This might be my favorite form of retargeting ad…and that is to offer upsells (or new products) to people who've already bought from me in the past.

And the reasoning is simple: the conversion rates on these types of ads are stupidly high. (And is probably the most profitable ROI you'll get from any kind of retargeting ad you run.)

That doesn't mean these types of ads are simple. (You can easily bug the ever-living crap out of your existing customers with too many of these.)

But if done properly, it can be some of the most impactive advertising you can do for your entire business.

Here's what to keep in mind about these upsell/new product retargeting ads:

- **Segment your customer base**

(first!) and then create your retargeting ad. Not all your customers are gonna be interested in every damn thing you must sell. Do your best to segment them out, either through filtered email lists or Facebook custom audience based on user behavior, so your ad is relevant and timely for your customers.

- **The best upsells are always related to your existing product** — and make things faster/easier/more customized for your consumer. This is a strategy that took me forever to figure out. (Unfortunately.) But you want the upsell to seem like a "no-brainer" proposition. Just ask folks if they'd like help getting your product or service set up. Or if they want personal attention from you or your team. (A good portion of your customer base will want this. So why not let them pay for it?)

- **Videos seem to work best with these types of ads.** In which you provide more information, and hammer home the benefits they'll be getting if they take advantage of the offer.

- **Try to add an urgent time limit if you can.** This isn't always possible but if you stress the offer is gonna expire in 7 days — and you really hope they take advantage of the opportunity before it goes away — you'll get a much higher conversion rate.

- **Just like with other retargeting ads, keep the frequency to about 15-20 times per month.** (And don't hammer your customers with the same ad for more than 30 days.)

- **This same process can work for freebie opt-ins,** where you're trying to your customers to pre-qualify themselves for a new email list. In that case a text ad that links directly to a landing page will work just fine.

Cool Ninja Facebook Retargeting Method #5: Reduce Refunds (With a Shout-Out to Current Customers)

This is a strategy I hit upon by accident. (Found it while helping a client who had a profitable coaching package but couldn't get his refund rate down.)

So, we created a simple Facebook retargeting ad — targeted at NEW coaching clients — that just said: "Thanks so much for checking out the coaching package. If ya got any questions, don't hesitate to ask."

And guess what…his refund rate dropped by 50%. (Considering his packages cost $1000/month, $1/day wasn't too bad an investment in ads.)

These do not have to be elaborate. Or time-consuming to create.

But if you've got an issue with refunds — especially for higher-ticket stuff — then I encourage giving these a try.

Here's what worked for my client:

- **Start with "Thank You."** Just having a banner ad that said "Thank You for Joining the Program" cut my client's refunds by half. (And the ad didn't offer anything else…just a message of thanks.)

- **Tell 'em you want them to succeed — and you KNOW they'll succeed.** Studies have shown the biggest reason people refund stuff isn't because they don't like the product…it's that they don't feel it'll work for THEM. (Or that they'll ever figure out how to use it.) So, just allay these fears and give 'em a nice encouraging nod forward.

- **The more expensive your product/service, the more complicated these should be**. In fact, for my client selling the coaching packages, we created a series of follow-up weekly videos that would check-in and see how people are doing. (You do this by segmenting customers into email lists that designate what week they're in a program — and then creating Facebook custom audiences based on those lists.)
- **These kinds of ads work even**

with folks who REFUNDED your product. Instead of getting bitter and angry, just create a simple ad thanking folks for giving the product a try and ask them if they'd fill out a survey about their experience. (You will learn more about your marketing funnel this way then 10K in consultancy fees.)

Cool Ninja Facebook Retargeting Method #6: Reach out to Warm Customers…Who've Grown Oh-So-Cold

We've gone over different ways you can use retarget to would-be and existing customers on Facebook. But this LAST one might be the most lucrative because you're simply re-energizing an asset you already have…but can't seem to figure out what the hell to do with.

How do you get your once red-hot customer base — that has suddenly grown colder than a hockey rink? Well, here's how I do it:

- **Decide on HOW you want to reach out your "once-awesome" customer base.** Do you want to offer them a special coupon or discount? Offer them a freebie? (Insider guides and free consulting works well.) Or maybe just ask them to fill out a survey so you can figure out how better to serve them.

- **Segment your existing email list,** or customer database, into a manageable asset based on a determining factor of your choosing. I generally like to target folks who haven't opened one of my emails in 3 months or so. But you may have a different set of factors you'd like to target. (Such as folks who haven't upgraded their software or downloaded your latest app.) Whatever it is, you gotta segment them in some way that Facebook can understand.

- **Create your ad and upload your customer data to create a Facebook custom audience.** I generally like to run these types of ads for a limited amount of time — usually for a week or so — every couple months. That way you don't over-saturate these folks.

And don't get too overwhelmed by all the options I've outlined here. (These are just possible retargeting directions you can go in. You don't have to employ each single one.)

But the cool thing about these retargeting campaigns is you can extend that chance to make the sale weeks, if not months, beyond initial contact. (Which can put unexpected

windfalls of money into your pocket.)

And speaking of putting money in your pocket, in the next chapter we're gonna cover some of the more advanced ninja Facebook marketing tools and tricks you can use to not only exponentially grow your bottom line — but automate much of this Facebook marketing "stuff."

Chapter Nine Key Takeaways:

- **Retargeting is the process where you "follow" visitors to your website** — through tracking code — so you can market to them on Facebook, or most any other place on the Internet.

- **One of the simplest, though hardly used, forms of retargeting is to promote content you must existing customers and email subscribers.** (Not only does it help the SEO ranking of your content, but it also helps segment your audience for future marketing.)

- **One of the most common, and effective, forms of retargeting ads is to give folks who didn't opt-in to your email list ANOTHER chance to opt-in.**

(Adding testimonials or answering objections are great ways to use this form of ad.)

- **The most used — and "Big Brother-y" — form of remarketing is to follow shopping cart abandoners and give them one more chance to buy their stuff.** Keep the frequency to these types of ads to 15-20x per month, or else you risk pissing them off.

- **My favorite type of remarketing ad is the "upsell" or "new offer" to existing customers.** They've already bought from you — some very recently — and they are primed to buy more good stuff from you in the future.

- **Reducing refund rates is a cinch with remarketing.** Just create some "Thank for buying! Got any questions!" type ads to make sure your customers are feeling satisfied and confident in their abilities to use your product or service.

- **Perhaps the most ninja form of remarketing is to reach out to customers who haven't responded to any of your marketing messages lately.** You could offer them discounts, freebies — or simply ask them how you can help them. (If they don't take the bait…feel free to remove 'em from your tribe.)

Chapter 10: Contests, Offers and Facebook Live…Oh My!

"If you don't set goals, you can't regret not reaching them."

-Yogi Berra

This might be the most profitable part of this book.

Because this is where we leverage all the hard work we've done up to this point and create some rather cheap and easy customer funnel activities that directly affect our bottom line.

But you gotta do the prep work.

You must build your Fan Page and post regular, frequent content that gets people to answer insipid questions and offer their opinions on a variety of subjects…

…and you've got to get some ad campaigns going that bring in new fans, leads and paying customers. (And maybe even a couple of ads that reclaim older customers from your marketing salvage yard.

Because when you've got all that going, you'll have so much engagement and social activity around your Facebook page, you'll be in a perfect place to run out the three super-ninja Facebook weapons of marketing awesomeness:

- Contests
- Offers
- Facebook Live Events

Now, you could certainly try these out before you run your first ad, but I highly recommend you master running a couple successful (if cheap) ad campaigns — and have a Facebook page with at least 2,000 fans — before rolling these out.

These are powerful strategies that work best when you've got the infrastructure in place to make it happen.

So, let's dig right in and get started with the first pillar of my Trinity of Facebook Promotion Awesomeness, which is:

Facebook Promotion Awesomeness Pillar No. 1: Contests and Sweepstakes

I'm still amazed how popular Facebook contests are. (I don't get particularly jazzed about entering a photo contest to win a free smoothie, but I am not most people.)

Mostly, contests and sweepstakes can be an excellent way to not only build your fan base and spread the word about your product or service — but also add some nice profits to your P&L sheet.

But it helps to know the difference between a contest and a sweepstakes, and what you have to do with each of them, to comply with Facebook's terms of service.

So, here's the scoop on Sweepstakes:

- **What They Are?** Chance-based promotions or random drawings usually hosted on a Facebook tab or on a 3rd-party solution. (More on that later.)

- **Do They Work?** Oh yeah. Especially if the prize is cool.

- **How to Set Up?** Easy to set up. Especially with a third-party sweepstakes app from a company such as WishPond, just fill in the fields and publish on a Facebook custom app. (WishPond has a 15-day free trial. Plenty of time to give your contest a try.)

- **What info do you collect?** Entrants often fill out a single form, usually involving the submission of their name and email (and often location and a phone number for future text marketing).

- **Who to target?** The barrier to entry for a sweepstakes should be quite low, which leads to a bigger pool of entrants. (Be aware, some people will enter more than once. Just the way it is.)

- **What Should the Prize Be?** Anything that is relevant to your fanbase. And cool!

Best Practices:

- Keep the entry form simple and to the point.

- Have good pictures of the prize on your landing page.

- Choose a sweepstakes app that has mobile capabilities. (Sweepstakes spread super quickly through mobile devices.)

- Keep the sweepstakes to about 5-7 days in length. (Longer than that and people will forget.)

Contests require a little more effort on the part of your fans, which can be good or bad.

Here's the skinny on Facebook Contests:

- **What They Are?** Contests are promotions where entrants must perform a specific action (such as upload a photo, write a caption, shoot a video, make a comment, dash off a quick essay.) to win a specified prize.

- **Do They Work?** Exceptionally well. When people go to the trouble of creating "something" for a contest, they often share it with all of their friends. (This stuff can spread REALLY fast.)

- **How to Set Up?** Just like a Facebook sweepstakes, you'll want to set up through a third-party app, such as WishPond. Let them handle the technical and legal crap that goes with setting up a contest.

- **What Should I Ask People to Do to Enter?** Well, there are tons of different ways to go here. You could ask people to: like your page, comment on a post, leave a photo caption, write a fill-in-the-blank, answer a Q&A…even crowdsource something. (Such as your new creative design or product idea.)

- **What Info Do You Collect?** Same as the sweepstakes. Name and email, at a minimum, and then location and phone number if you have a plan to use it. (Don't ask for more than that.)

- **Who to Target?** Whomever you think will act and enter the contest. Will retirees in Phoenix upload their Instagram photos from their latest Friday night? Probably not. But goth teenagers might.

- **What Should the Prize Be?** Not only relevant, but something commensurate with the effort required for the contest. If you're asking people to write an essay, you need to offer them more than a Slurpee coupon.

Best Practices:

- Make sure to create ads around your contests. (I love video ads for these. Helps you get your message out there — and get new entrants.)

- Make the entry form SUPER CLEAR about what's needed to win. (Unclear contest guidelines can lead to huge headaches.)

- Like sweepstakes, make sure the app you use is mobile-friendly.

- All things being equal, go for photos over videos and captions over essays. (Make it easy, and more people will enter.)

- Create a separate email list for these entrants and create follow-up emails welcoming them to your tribe. Go easy on the soft sell. Wait till you've established a relationship.

- Keep the sweepstakes to about 5-7 days. (Longer than that and people will forget.)

Facebook Promotion Awesomeness Pillar No. 2: Offers

I hate to break it to ya…but 57% of all Facebook users like a brand or company for the "discounts and offers" they receive.

That means your fans are selfish. They don't love your brand, they love a great deal.

Which is why Facebook offers are so frickin' awesome. Here's how they work: (And yes! They still work!)

1. **Create an offer.** You can either do this straight from your page or from your Ads Manager.

2. **Promote your offer.** You can use many of the ad types we mentioned in the

previous chapters. (I especially like the Promoted Posts, Video Ads, and retargeting ads.)

3.   **Sit back and collect your money** as people redeem your offer.

One quick downside to Facebook offers is that you must have 400 fans for your page before you can start using them. (Or at least as of the writing of this book.) Otherwise these things totally rock.

So, what's so great about Facebook offers? Well…

- You can choose whether people redeem them online or print them out and redeem them in person. (Ideal for online and local businesses alike.)
- The offer is tied to the email address that the user has connected to Facebook with. (This means they'll get it and use it!) And it

won't be some spam filter email address.

- You can set a time limit for the offer.
- You can set up a quantity limit for the offer.
- If you promote with a page post ad, you can do some seriously cool location targeting. (This is awesome for local businesses.)
- The offer can show up in the newsfeed for maximum visibility.
- Promoting your offer can be surprisingly cheap. (Especially with all them different ad options we mentioned earlier.)

What kinds of stuff can you promote with a Facebook offer? Obviously, coupons and discounts work well.

But so do webinars, online trainings, video courses…pretty much anything where there is

something of high perceived value being offered at some kind of special price.

Here are a couple of tips when crafting your Facebook offer to get the most bang for your buck:

- **Get to the point in your copy.** You've only got 90 characters so no futzing around talking about the features. Get right to the deal and what people can expect to get from the deal. Example: "Click to receive 2-for-1 Pizza deal at New York Joe's."

- **Tell people to act.** "Click here," "Click now," "Download now," "Grab yours now..." Don't be shy. Tell 'em what to do.

- **Set up an initial budget of about $30-$40 to get started.** This will get you a ton of exposure if your targeting is halfway decent.

- **Always opt for dollars saved, over

percentage off. Which sounds better: "50% off all blazers at Macy's," or "Save $20 on a Macy's blazer today"? Specific always beats vague.

Facebook Promotion Awesomeness Pillar No. 3: Facebook Live!

So, why would we want to use Facebook Live? I mean, don't we want to just use YouTube for our video.

Well, first off, Facebook and YouTube are in a death struggle together to carve out video share. And that Facebook Live is…well…live means you could use it to stream video of your:

- Live events
- Product launches
- Behind-the-scenes looks at your business (Such a meet-the-team video)

- Weekly (or daily) how-to tip
- Webinars or seminars
- Coaching programs
- Q&As (I think these could be powerful)
- Breaking news

There's a reason Facebook is paying content partners like the New York Times to create content specifically for Facebook Live. (And those guys in Silicon Valley pay for anything they don't have to.)

They want to create unique, live content that is exclusive to their platform. (And I believe they will go to great lengths to promote it.)

So, if you're already doing a weekly blog — or monthly article/column — I would encourage you to focus all that energy on frequent Facebook Live offering.

Not only will it help establish you as an authority to your existing tribe and future customers, but I suspect that Facebook will give you some same promotional push they give to media stalwarts like

The New York Times.

Which, if nothing else, is an awesome trivia question you can share at parties: "Guess what me and The New York Times have in common?"

Chapter 10 Key Takeaways:

- **Set up a sweepstakes or contest using a 3rd-party app, such as WishPond, to give away a cool prize** relevant to your business, and don't forget to make it mobile compatible.

- **Good ideas for contests include** having folks like your page, make a comment on a post, answer a Q&A, leave a photo caption…or anything cool that you can think of.

- **Yes, offers still work!** Especially if you've got one that sounds irresistible. Just create an offer and promote it through Facebook ads. Have your copy get to the point and don't forget "dollars off" usually sounds better than "% off."

- **Facebook Live is awesome for

broadcasting your live events, Q&As and weekly how-to content — anything that lets you talk to the peeps in real-time. (Maybe even…like..sell something.)

Epilogue: If You Don't Like the Weather...

You could spend months, if not years, trying to become a Facebook expert.

Don't.

It's just not worth it.

The (somewhat) Draconian rules and regulations that Facebook forces upon its ~~victims~~ advertisers can be changed at any moment. (Without any warning.)

And that Fan Page community you've spent years cultivating can suddenly disappear because Facebook changed its quantum affinity algorithm flux capacitor and you're left out in the Status Update cold.

And, though I have done my best to brain dump

all the little ninja Facebook tricks and tactics I've learned the hard way (and at quite an expense)… minutes after I finish typing this epilogue, some of the things in here may already be obsolete.

Just remember that as many new little tools and tweaks and "you gotta have this one thing" service Facebook offers…

…the principles will never change.

Facebook is that kid's tree house in the backyard.

It's a place where people like to meet up with their friends, catch up on gossip…even get into a couple of arguments.

But it's their place. Their zone. Their home away from the parents.

And it's your job as a Facebook marketer to build that tree house.

To fill it with comic books and Barbie dolls and baseball cards and an EZ Bake Oven and let the kids just ramble on and have a great time and feel important and feel like this is the safest place in the world.

So, when you have a product or service you think they'd like, or would enjoy, or could possibly improve/change their lives…

They'll pounce on it. Because they trust the tree house. (And the person who built it.)

And though I'm straining metaphors here, I truly believe that (whether I like it or not) the only marketing that will survive in the competitive years ahead will be marketing that doesn't feel like marketing.

Selling that doesn't even remotely feel like selling.

Web properties that feel like tree houses.

Here's hoping this book provided a nail or two to help you build some tree houses for your business.

Good luck with your Facebook marketing, and if you'd like to drop me a line to tell me what you thought of this book, you can email me at michael@punkrockmarketing.com.

And if you've enjoyed this book, or even if you

didn't enjoy the book, would you be willing to leave a review?

Even a sentence or two really helps us indie authors carve out a career as a creative professional.

HEAD OVER to PunkRockMarketing.com/Fbook to leave a review on Amazon (and enjoy truckloads of good karma):

Oh, and just one more thing…

A Special FREE Gift for You!

If you'd like FREE instant access to my seminar "How to Make a Damn Good Living With Social Media (Even If You Hate Social Media" then head over to **PunkRockMarketing.com/Free**. (What else you gonna do? Watch another "Twilight" movie?!)

not intended as BUSINESS advice. 7Use of the programs, advice, and information contained in this book is at the sole choice and risk of the reader.

Made in the USA
Monee, IL
15 December 2019